ALLEN PHO

YOUR HC ... ILLIH

CONTENTS

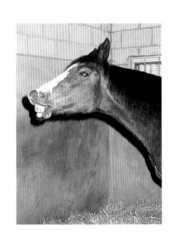

INTRODUCTION

The health of your horse's teeth is particularly important because the horse is a herbivore and trickle feeder. At times, when relying on grazing alone, it may need to eat for 20 hours out of 24 in order to satisfy its nutritional needs. Anything which interferes with the efficiency of this process – a covering of snow, too small an area for grazing, or an uncomfortable mouth – means that the animal could lose weight.

A comfortable mouth is not only in the interest of the horse's welfare but it is also important to the rider. Many behavioural or training problems may be related to mouth pain and if the pain is eradicated the problems disappear.

The teeth are also very useful as a means of estimating or confirming the age of a horse. When a horse is bought for a particular purpose, its age may be vitally important. A competition horse which has not won much as a five- or six-year-old but shows promise is worth much more than a horse of apparently similar ability at nine or ten years. A small child's pony in its late teens may be suitable for a youngster learning to ride who will soon outgrow the pony but not for an older child who wants to improve and compete at increasingly high levels over a number of years.

NORMAL TEETH

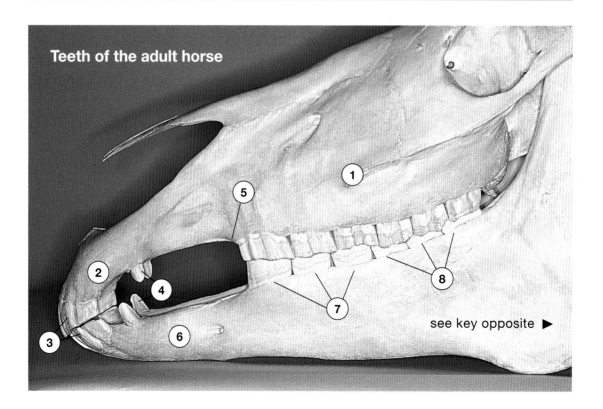

Teeth of the adult horse

see key opposite ▶

In the adult horse of five years and older, a full set of adult teeth consists of three pairs of **incisors** in each jaw – the *centrals*, *laterals* and *corners* – and six pairs of cheek teeth or **molars**. In addition there may be a pair of **canines** or **tushes** (*see right*) in males (sometimes small or vestigial in females).

> **WARNING**
>
> Horses are capable of biting off fingers! Great care must always be taken when inserting fingers or a hand into a horse's mouth.

Cheek teeth (**molars** and **premolars**) are large grinding teeth with a fairly rectangular surface, although the first and last in each row are three-sided. The **exposed crown** is about 2 cm above the gum in the young adult horse and the **reserve crown** is around 6 cm below the gum (*see below*). Each tooth has two deep **infundibulae** lined with enamel so that the wearing surface shows slightly raised convoluted lines of hard enamel. The distance between the two upper rows of cheek teeth is slightly wider than the two bottom rows so that the upper ones slightly overhang the lower ones on the outside and are tight up against the cheek. Similarly, the inside edges of the lower teeth are not covered by the upper teeth so these edges can become sharp and require rasping.

Key: teeth of the adult horse

1. maxilla
2. premaxilla
3. incisors
4. canines
5. (site of) wolf tooth
6. lower jaw or mandible
7. premolars
8. molars

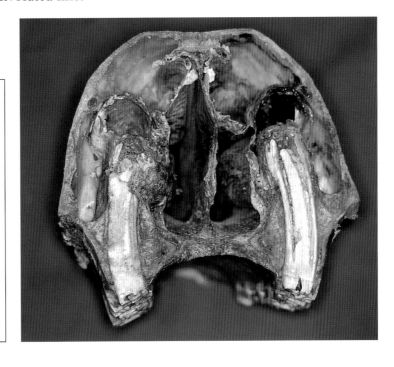

Some horses also have **wolf teeth**. These are small premolars just in front of the main cheek teeth. They may be absent or only present in the maxilla (colloquially, but technically incorrectly, referred to as the upper **jawbone**). They are permanent teeth but have little root, so are easy to knock out. They vary considerably in size from a tiny stump to, occasionally, 20 mm or more. Long ones are thought to cause bitting problems and are generally removed in a simple swift operation by a veterinary surgeon. They can cause head shaking and riding problems, but sometimes are wrongly blamed for these problems, which can have a variety of other causes.

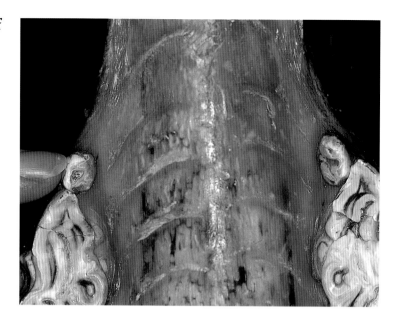

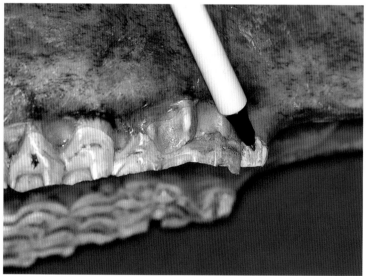

The incisors are for grazing – tearing and cutting at grass – and the molars are grinding teeth. Originally dentition was roughly similar in all mammals, and evolution has caused some teeth to become vestigial; the canines (tushes) and wolf teeth no longer serve any useful purpose in the horse. There is a convenient gap between the incisors and the molars known as a **diastema** on both sides of the upper and lower jaw. In the lower jaw, the bit of a bridled horse lies on the gums of these gaps, which are commonly known as the **bars** of the mouth.

TEMPORARY AND PERMANENT TEETH

The first three molars are generally referred to as premolars as they are present in both the temporary and permanent dentition, whereas the back three are permanent only. Tushes and wolf teeth are also only present in the permanent dentition. Incisors are both temporary and permanent.

Temporary teeth may also be referred to as deciduous or milk teeth. The **temporary incisors** have a curved outline going into a neck where they enter the gum, and a small root. The **permanent incisors** become narrower towards the gum but are straight-sided. They have a long reserve crown within the gum which gradually advances from the **alveolus** (socket) throughout the horse's life as the tooth wears away.

The top photo shows permanent incisors (*left*) and temporary incisors (*right*).

Temporary premolars have little reserve crown and are pushed out by the permanent molars erupting underneath them. They sit on top of the permanent molars and are eventually dislodged and fall out as **molar caps** between the ages of 18 months and four years.

The middle photo shows premolar caps. The bottom photo shows premolar caps (*left*) and permanent molar (*right*).

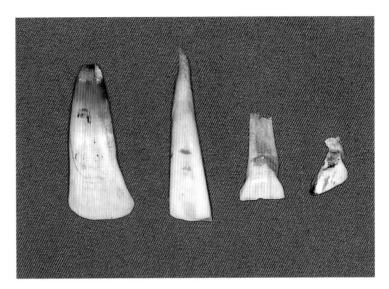

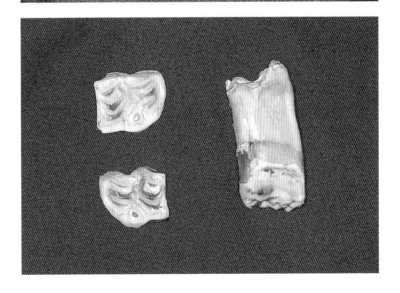

TOOTH STRUCTURE

The longitudinal section of an incisor tooth is of particular interest as it enables us to understand how the **tables** or **occlusal surfaces** of the tooth are helpful in ageing horses. The tooth has a thin outer layer of **cementum** which is mostly worn away to reveal the hard white **enamel** layer (0.5–1.0 mm thick). In the centre of the tooth is a deep hollow known as the **infundibulum**. This is surrounded by another layer of enamel which takes some ten years to wear away and so is a useful guide to age. The hole is partially filled with cementum. Coming up from the bottom of the tooth is the **pulp cavity** (dental star) and this overlaps the infundibulum. The remainder of the tooth is filled with **dentine**. All these features mean that as the tooth wears away, a different pattern is revealed by the cross-section as it reaches the wearing surface.

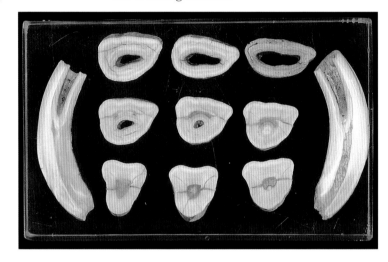

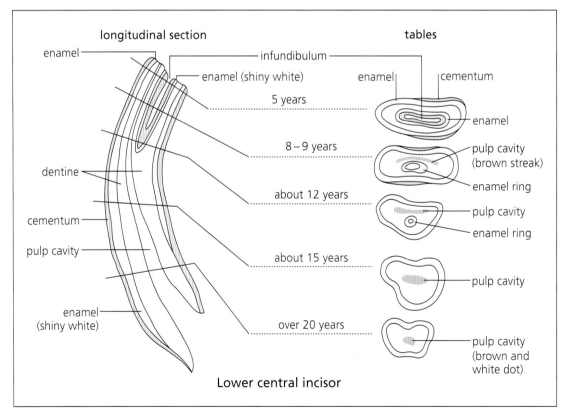

Lower central incisor

AGEING THE HORSE

The reason the teeth may be used to determine a horse's age is that they are continually growing and being worn away. As the tooth wears down, its cross-section changes in shape and the pattern of features on its surface changes.

The official birthday of all registered Thoroughbreds in the Northern hemisphere is the first of January. This was originally chosen so that horses would not change their age during the flat-racing season which, before the recent introduction of all-weather tracks, was restricted to between March and October. The official breeding season for Thoroughbreds is 15 February to 15 July and so all Thoroughbred foals are likely to be born from mid-January to mid-June (gestation in the mare averages 340 days). Horses are seasonal breeders and so most non-Thoroughbred foals will be born between April and July. Traditionally then, Thoroughbreds change their age on the first of January, non-Thoroughbred breeds on the first of May. Southern-hemisphere horses will usually be born in their springtime, that is, between October and January, and there the official birthday for racing Thoroughbreds is the first of August.

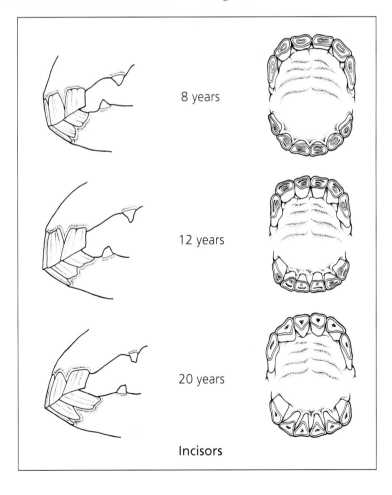

8 years

12 years

20 years

Incisors

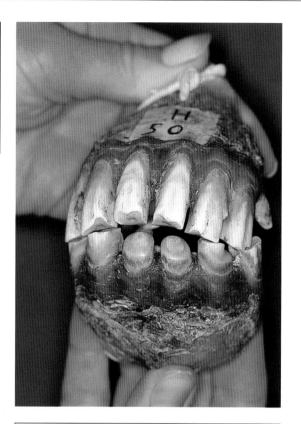

POINTS TO BEAR IN MIND

The degree of wear and the rate of development of the teeth will vary according to the breeding of the animal and the environment in which it has been kept. The degree of variation increases with age. Hot-blooded horses (Thoroughbreds and Arabs) tend to mature earlier than the larger, heavier breeds. Ponies from mountains and moorlands grazing tough or sparse grassland are likely to show more wear to their incisor teeth than horses which are stabled and fed concentrate feeds and hay. Horses with misaligned teeth (*see right*) or **crib-biters** will show unusual patterns of wear.

GALVAYNE'S GROOVE

Sidney Galvayne was an Australian horseman who came to England at the end of the nineteenth century. He wrote a book entitled *Horse Dentition* and described a feature of the upper corner incisor which he named Galvayne's Groove. This groove

appears on the side of the tooth at the gum edge when the horse is 10 years old and reaches the bottom of the tooth at around 20 years. It then disappears between 20 and 30 years and the tooth has a more rounded outline.

The horses shown here are 15 years old (*right*) and 18 years old (*below*).

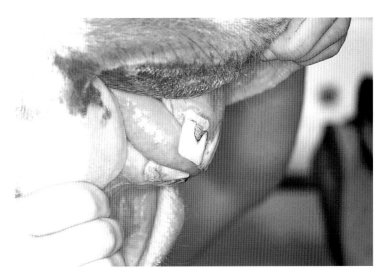

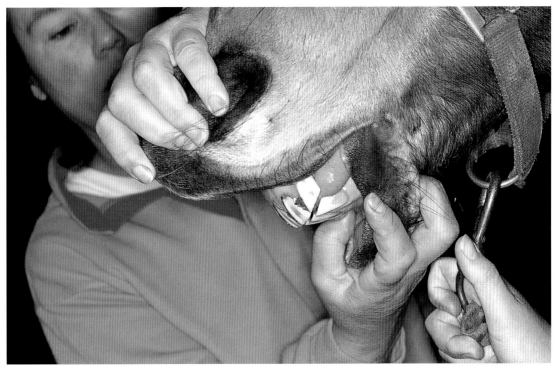

CAUTION

It is often difficult to see precisely where the groove starts and finishes. Younger horses sometimes will show a similar groove. It is therefore a useful addition to other factors when ageing horses but should not be relied upon on its own.

HOW TO DECIDE YOUR HORSE'S AGE

Firstly, take a general look at the animal and decide whether it is in its youth (under 5 years), middle age (5–15 years) or old age (over 15 years). Do not allow yourself to be hurried. Take all the factors outlined so far into consideration: breed, past lifestyle and general background.

Youth   The animal will be of babyish, immature appearance, with long legs, upright pasterns, the quarters often higher than the withers, short mouth and bushy tail.

1year   Irish draught x Thoroughbred ►

Middle age   The animal will be of mature proportions, fully developed and with a few signs of wear and tear.

12 years   Heavy horse – Shire cross ►

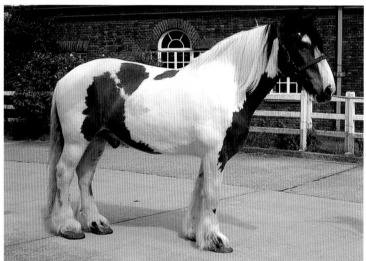

Old age   The animal may show increasing signs of wear and tear, such as scars or distended joints or tendons. It may show some greying of the coat and muzzle if of dark colour, and may be haggard, with a sway back, over at the knee, and have hooded eyes.

20 years   Thoroughbred ►

Secondly, confirm your decision by looking at the general appearance of the teeth. Do this by gently drawing back the lips. There is no need to draw the tongue out at this stage.

Youth Some or all of the teeth are temporary, and will look 'shelly', very white, and show a 'neck' between crown and root. Permanent teeth may be cut or cutting but there is little sign of wear. The incisors meet at an angle approaching 180 degrees. The incisor tables are oval and much wider from side to side than from front to back.

Middle age The horse has a full mouth of permanent teeth in wear. The incisors meet at an increasingly acute angle depending on age, and the enamel ring surrounding the infundibulum is still visible on some or all of the lower tables. The tables become more triangular.

Old age The teeth are often yellowish and stained, sometimes showing damage or **dental calculus**. The incisors meet at an acute angle (less than 90 degrees). The infundibulum has gone from all the lower incisors, apart from perhaps a trace in the corners, and only the pulp cavity (dental star) can be seen, which has become centralised. The tables become square and then wider from front to back than from side to side in very old horses.

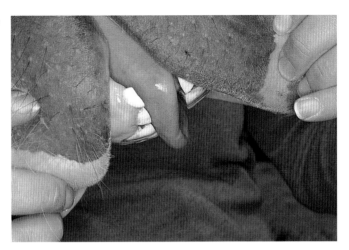

3½ years

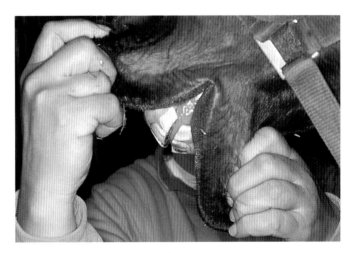

7½ years

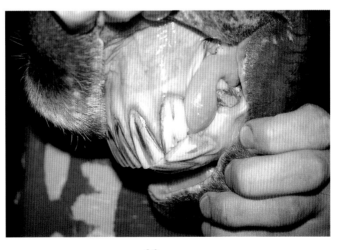

30 years

Thirdly, examine the incisors methodically. This can usually be done by inserting a hand through the diastema (gap) between the incisors and molars and grasping the tongue. Often it is sufficient just to press back the tongue or roll it up, but alternatively it can be gently drawn out to one side. *Do not use the tongue to restrain the horse.* In awkward cases, it may be necessary to use a Swale's gag (see page 22).

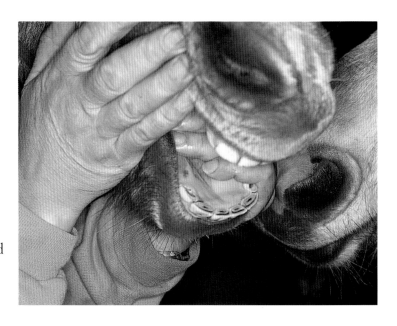

The foal is born with its first pair of temporary incisors just cut. During the first year, the laterals are cut at 4–6 weeks along with the premolars, and the corners at 9 months. A yearling will have the corner incisors just meeting, by 18 months they are half worn and by 2 years they are worn over the whole surface. The wolf tooth, if present, appears at about 6 months.

The temporary premolars are present soon after birth and the molars (the back three cheek teeth) erupt at 9 months, 18 months and around 3½ years.

The permanent incisors take about 6 months from just coming through the gum to fully up and showing a smooth surface of wear. The temporary pairs are replaced at 2½ years (centrals), 3½ years (laterals) and 4½ years (corners) respectively.

At 5 years the horse has a full mouth and the corner incisors have met along the front edges, but the back corner is still rounded and unworn.

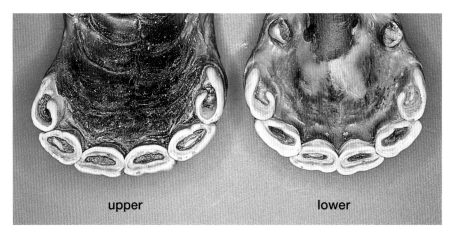

upper   lower

5 years

At 6 years old, the corner incisors have lost their curled shell-like appearance and are in wear over about half of their surface, but there is little wear on the back edges of the upper ones or the inside edges of the lower ones. Tushes in the male are well developed and pointed with sharp edges.

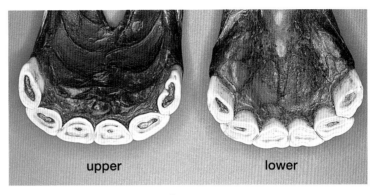

upper   lower

7 years

At 7 years old in the central incisors the ring of enamel is long but the cup or hollow in the middle of it may have filled in and the pulp cavity starts to appear in front of the infundibulum as a brown streak. The other lower incisors generally still have hollow cups. The upper corner incisor commonly has a softly rounded hook on its posterior edge due to it overhanging the lower one (**7-year hook**).

The photographs here show a 7-year hook (*below*) and a hook at 16 years (*right*).

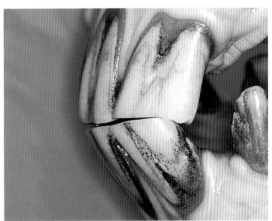

16 years

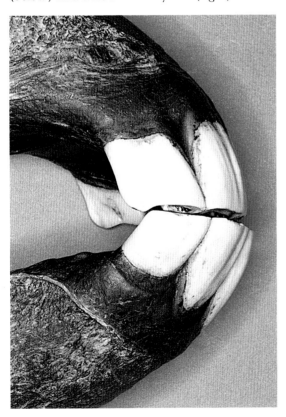

7 years

CAUTION

Hooks on the upper corner incisor can appear at any age and should not be used as the sole means of ageing the horse. The only fairly reliable hook is the 7-year hook which has a smooth outline and a large hollow infundibulum in the tooth. The opposing lower incisor will not be in wear over the whole surface. Even so, animals between 6 and 8 can show this hook.

Between 7 and 13 years a number of changes take place. Look at the table of the central lower incisor; the changes here happen about a year later in the laterals and two years later in the corners.

The shape of the tooth changes from oval to triangular to square. The infundibulum changes from long at 7 years, to egg-shaped at 9 years, to circular at 11 years, disappearing at 13 years. The pulp cavity develops from a brown streak anterior to the infundibulum to a brown and white dot nearer the centre of the table in a slight depression. Remember, the infundibulum is characterised by a raised ring of enamel which may be felt by running a finger-nail across it.

The photographs show teeth at 9 years (*top*), 11 years (*centre*) and 15 years (*right*).

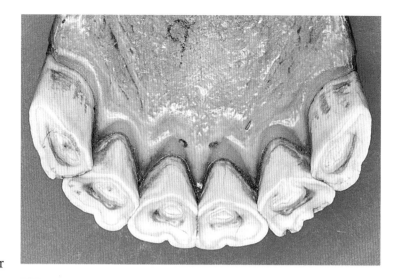

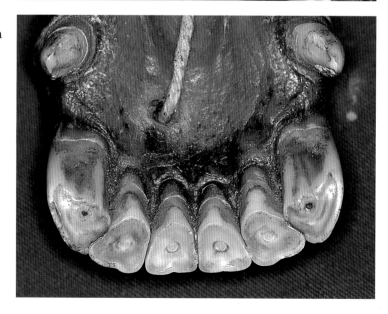

Between 13 and 16 years the enamel of the infundibulum disappears in turn from each pair of lower incisors so that by 16 years there will only be the brown and white dot of the pulp cavity. Occasionally a trace of enamel will persist. The incisor tables will be square by this time. Galvayne's Groove, if visible, will be making its way down the outside of the upper corner incisor, often stained brown, it should be half way down by 15 years. The upper incisors would still show clear infundibular rings with hollows at 16 years.

Between 16 and 20 years the hollows in the upper infundibulae fill in and the enamel rings become more circular and faint. The angle at which the teeth meet approaches 90 degrees and the tables become longer from front to back than from side to side. Galvayne's Groove should reach the bottom by 20 years. The gums begin to recede.

Between 20 and 25 years the rings of enamel on the upper incisor tables disappear. The lower **arcade** (alignment of the row of incisors) is less curved than in young horses and each table is longer from front to back. The gums continue to recede and the horse appears 'long in the tooth'. Horses of this age should not be in hard work, though many ponies are fit to continue longer.

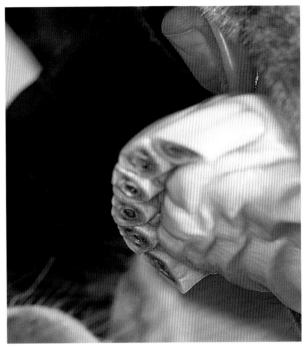

16 years

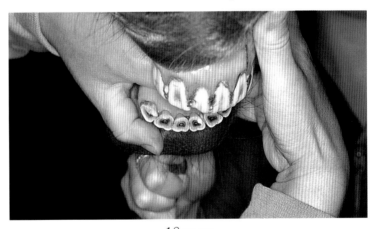

18 years

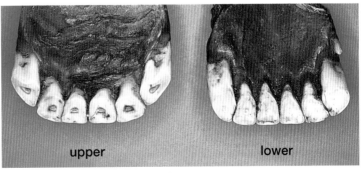

upper   lower

25 years

Horses over 25 years will have teeth meeting at an acute angle with an almost straight arcade. There is unlikely to be any infundibulum showing on top or bottom tables although in ponies it may persist longer. The corner tooth appears rounded with the disappearance of Galvayne's Groove between 20 and 30 years. Horses of this age are generally retired and few reach the age of 30.

It is exceptional for horses to live to be over 30 years, and they are difficult to age accurately. Their condition is of more importance and they should receive careful feeding as their teeth may be very worn and they may have difficulty grazing.

The pony shown here (*above and below*) is over 30 years old.

PROBLEM TEETH

Fortunately, serious problems with horses' teeth are relatively rare but there are a number of minor problems which can easily be attended to. The owner may be alerted to these by noticing the horse **quidding** (spitting out half-chewed forage), losing condition or having difficulty eating. There may be a problem which shows itself when the horse is ridden, such as head-shaking, bit evasion or one-sidedness. There may also be foul-smelling breath, nasal discharge or facial swelling.

MALOCCLUSION

Malocclusion (poor alignment) of the teeth may cause problems. An *overshot* jaw or sow mouth means that the lower teeth come further forward than the upper ones. This is rare in horses. An *undershot* jaw or *parrot mouth* (*see right*) is one where the upper teeth overhang the lower teeth. In either case the fact that the teeth do not meet may cause difficulty in grazing and by failing to wear against each other they may become uneven or overlong if not regularly rasped. Such horses may be fine if given hay and concentrate feed. Where cheek

teeth are damaged, missing or not meeting properly the opposing tooth may become overlong or uneven. This is sometimes termed *step mouth* or *wavy mouth* and can usually be controlled by regular rasping (see p. 18).

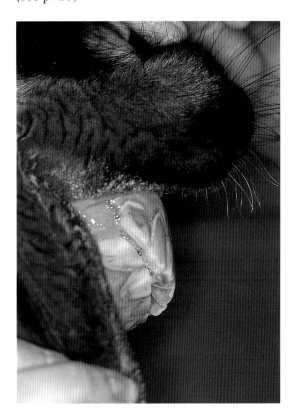

WOLF TEETH

Wolf teeth, as previously mentioned, may cause bitting and riding problems, and should be removed if this is suspected. A circular wolf tooth extractor or a special chisel is used. Wolf teeth should not be confused with the tushes, which are canine teeth.

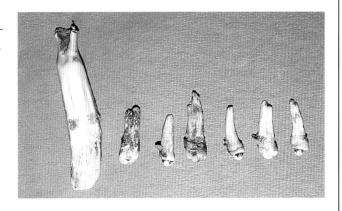

SHARP CHEEK TEETH

These are a very common problem. The outside edges of the upper ones and the inside edges of the lower ones become sharp with wear because of the way in which they meet. Sometimes they become so sharp that they can cut or ulcerate the cheeks or tongue and care should be taken when examining them with a hand. The edges may easily be rasped off during a routine dental check. Some horses may need this every six months, others seldom or never. It is best to check them annually, perhaps when your veterinary surgeon is vaccinating your horse.

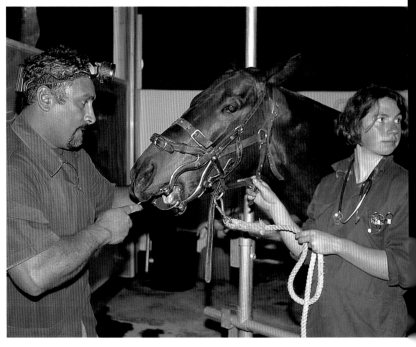

Enamel hooks can develop on the first or last cheek tooth and these can be rasped off or cut off with a special instrument. Care must be taken particularly with the back teeth not to damage the sensitive tissues beyond them and for this reason hook cutters are often used rather than rasps.

RETAINED TEMPORARY TEETH

Premolar caps are the remains of temporary premolars which sit on top of the permanent teeth and are gradually pushed out. Usually they fall out by themselves and are sometimes found in the manger. They may also fall out when a young horse of 2–4 years old is having its teeth rasped. Racehorses in training are generally checked to see that they have not become stuck or are causing eating difficulties. If they are causing discomfort then they may be removed but premature removal could leave the pulp exposed to infection.

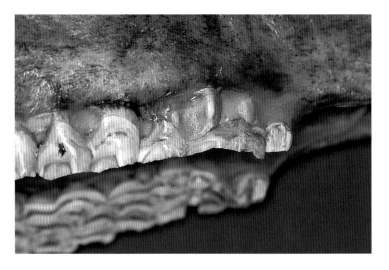

Retained temporary incisors are fairly common where the permanent tooth has come through and failed to push out the deciduous one. Usually they are loose enough to pull out with the fingers or forceps (*see right*). Sedation and local anaesthetic may be necessary.

Supernumary teeth may cause crowding problems so that the teeth overlap and do not meet properly. It may be necessary to remove one or more of the teeth to allow space or rasp any that are being unevenly worn.

DECAY AND OTHER PROBLEMS

Decay is not common in horses because of their diet but can occur, particularly where there has been tooth damage and the pulp has been exposed. This may lead to an abscess which may manifest as pain, swelling and a thick nasal or facial discharge. This is a job for a veterinary surgeon and may need radiography and surgery but in some cases can be treated by a prolonged

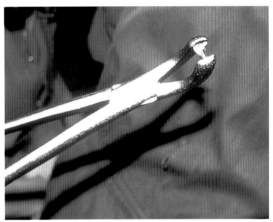

course of antibiotics. **Periodontitis** (infection around the teeth, such as gum disease) can also be caused by food pocketing in older horses where teeth are displaced or missing. In younger horses this is often transient during permanent tooth eruption and resolves of its own accord.

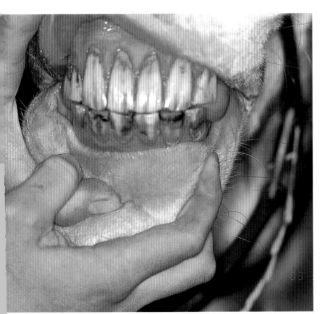

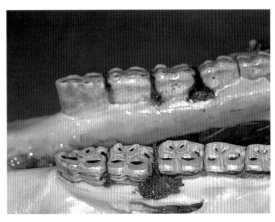

Impaction and displacement may occur where there is insufficient space for the teeth. This is particularly a problem in very small equines such as Shetlands or Falabellas, where the mouth is too small to accommodate all the cheek teeth. Food can become caught up in the cheeks, and cysts and then abscesses may form. Some teeth may have to be removed under general anaesthetic.

Three-year bumps visible on the outside of the lower jaw (*top photo*) are normal when molars are erupting.

Dental calculus is an encrustation of mineralised material which sometimes accumulates on the incisors or tushes. It does not generally cause much problem although the gums may be a little inflamed. It is softish and can easily be removed with forceps or dental elevators.

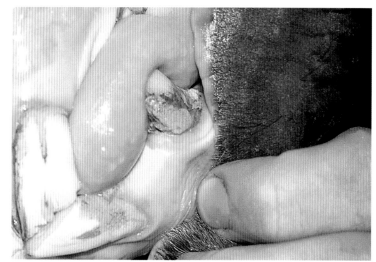

Crib-biting and **crib-whetting** are stereotypies which can cause damage to the incisors by abnormal wear. This may not have much effect on the horse's grazing ability until it is quite old but it does make ageing the horse with accuracy difficult.

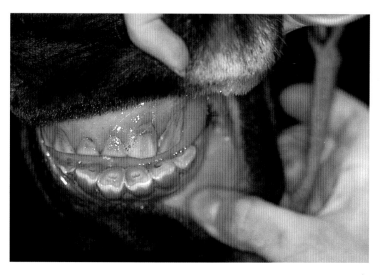

THE HORSE DENTIST

THE VETERINARY SURGEONS' ACT 1966

Under this act of Parliament only qualified veterinary surgeons may diagnose, carry out surgery, and prescribe drugs to animals. There are a few exceptions where an owner may do certain things to his own animal or in life-threatening emergencies. All such activities are controlled by the Protection of Animals Act 1911 and subsequent legislation on welfare and the prevention of cruelty.

The term 'dentist' may only legally be used by persons registered with the British Dental Association. Very occasionally, a veterinary surgeon will also be a qualified (human) dentist. Dental technicians are lay people who may be very expert in what they do but at present are restricted to certain procedures; for example they may rasp a horse's teeth but they may not administer sedation or anaesthetic or carry out an extraction involving surgery. At present anyone may unofficially call themselves an 'equine dentist'. Some of these people are very skilled and experienced and may have qualifications from such bodies as the World Wide Association of Equine Dentistry, or they may have no training at all.

The British Equine Veterinary Association and the British Veterinary Dental Association are proposing to rationalise the situation and ultimately to hold courses, examinations and registration for all those practising veterinary dentistry. Reputable dental technicians generally work closely with veterinary surgeons.

RESTRAINT

Most horses are remarkably tolerant of having their teeth examined and rasped. It is best to have the animal in stocks or backed into the corner of a large loose box. It should wear a head collar with a loose noseband so that it is able to open its mouth without restriction. Although it is possible to carry out minor procedures without a gag it is probably easier and more efficient to use one. The commonest gags are **Haussman**'s and **Swale**'s.

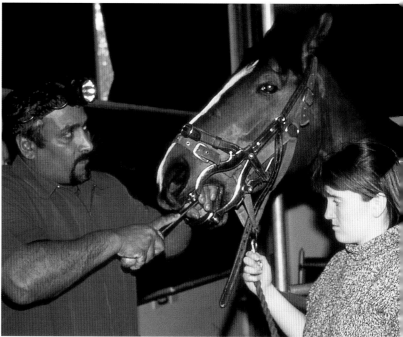

Haussman's gag (*see top photo*) has the advantage that it leaves the molars free on both sides but it obscures the incisors. It is rather cumbersome to insert but very secure once in position.

Swale's gag (*see right*) is easier to insert but relies on the molars on one side biting onto it to hold the mouth open. It can however be put in on either side. Care should be taken when removing a gag not to knock it against the teeth, which can make the horse more difficult on a future occasion.

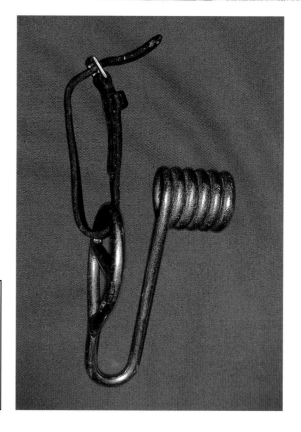

SEDATION

For difficult horses or for tricky procedures sedation may be necessary and this must be administered by a veterinary surgeon. The same applies to local anaesthesia.

INSTRUMENTS

The most commonly used instrument will be a **rasp** (*see right*). There are manual and mechanical ones of different lengths and with their heads set at different angles.

Enamel hooks may be removed with **hook cutters** or **dental shears** and wolf teeth removed with a special cylindrical **dental elevator** (*see below, right*).

EXTRACTIONS

These may only be carried out by a veterinary surgeon. The removal of wolf teeth and retained deciduous teeth may be done under sedation with the horse standing, but all other extractions require a general anaesthetic. The removal of molars is a major undertaking which can have complications. The tooth is usually repulsed from the apex (pushed out from the root) by a surgical incision into the side of the face and the removal of a piece of bone. Careful post-operative nursing is essential to prevent infection.

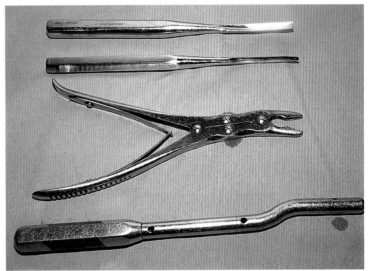

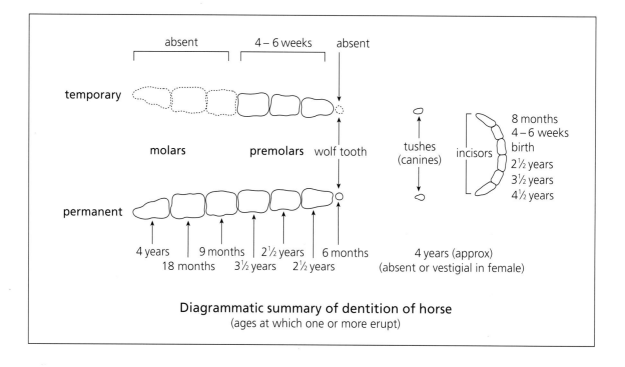

Diagrammatic summary of dentition of horse
(ages at which one or more erupt)

ACKNOWLEDGEMENTS

I would like to thank my colleagues and students at the Cambridge University Veterinary School, everyone who allowed me to photograph their animals, Joe Collins, Col. J. Hickman, Gary Singh-Khakhian, and most of all Susan Beer and Mouldy!

British Library Cataloguing-in-Publication Data.
A catalogue record for this book is available from the British Library

ISBN 0.85131.751.0

Published in Great Britain in 1999
J. A. Allen an imprint of Robert Hale Ltd.,
Clerkenwell House, 45–47 Clerkenwell Green,
London EC1R 0HT

Design and Typesetting by Paul Saunders
Edited by Susan Beer
Series editor Jane Lake
Colour processing by Tenon & Polert Colour Processing Ltd., Hong Kong
Printed in Hong Kong by Dah Hua International Printing Press Co. Ltd.